MEN DON'T DIE FOR A LIE

How the Resurrection Still Matters to You

Monsignor James B. Reynolds

Edited and compiled by Kathleen M. Hackett

Copyright © 2026 Kathleen Hackett

Sermons © Estate of Monsignor James B. Reynolds

All rights reserved.

ISBN: 9798245097893

ISBN- Independently published

Imprimatur:
    ✠ Thomas G. Wenski
    Archbishop of Miami
    Miami, Florida
    February 2, 2026

Dedication

This book is dedicated to the memory of Monsignor James B. Reynolds, the Reynolds descendants of the Dinsmore and Hackett Families and to all of the Apostles and Disciples who were martyred or died for believing in the

Resurrection and Good News of Jesus Christ.

Table Of Contents

FOREWORD v

CHAPTER ONE - SING YOUR HEART OUT 1

CHAPTER TWO - OUR REDEEMER LIVES 8

CHAPTER THREE - MORE THAN WISHFUL THINKING 16

CHAPTER FOUR - DO MEN DIE FOR A LIE? 23

CHAPTER FIVE - EVERY DAY A LITTLE BIT 28

CHAPTER SIX - ARE YOU LISTENING?.......36

CHAPTER SEVEN - THIS TREMENDOUS LOVER..44

CHAPTER EIGHT - ARE WE ALL SUNK?.....52

CHAPTER NINE - A PRICELESS GIFT..........60

CHAPTER TEN - DEATH IS DEATH.............70

CHAPTER ELEVEN - DIVINE GOSSIP 79

CHAPTER TWELVE - FEELINGS 86

   AFTERWORD...93

   ACKNOWLEDGEMENT 103

Foreword

Most of us have experienced listening to a lecture, speech, presentation, or sermon (homily). Sometimes we catch only a small snippet of what was said that has "staying power" in our minds. Often a catch phrase, particular story or theme resonates within us and stays as a permanent reminder of where, when, and how we heard it. Or it is but a fleeting thought, in one ear, out the other. Then there are times you wish you could hold onto the entire message, word for word, so you can reread, devour, and absorb what was so brilliantly professed.

In our highly technological age here in 2026, cell phones easily record audio or video for instant replays. Systems exist now for creating and archiving data at the touch of a button. Now Artificial Intelligence (AI) can generate entire books in seconds. But years ago, not so far away, the only thing available was a Royal typewriter, a blank sheet of paper, and white correction tape. Those were the tools my uncle Monsignor James B. Reynolds, (Monsignor Jim) used to compile his sermons for seventy years. He even used the blank page of unused Sunday Bulletins to type his reflections.

Upon his death on February 28, 2022, at the age of 97, I joined three of my six cousins to help with the duty of clearing his condo in Pompano Beach, Florida. It is there that we discovered a treasure trove of all his sermons neatly filed according to the Roman Catholic liturgical calendars dating back to his ordination time June 3, 1950. The question arose, keep or toss? I couldn't bring myself to discard seventy years of prayer, thought, and faith. So, I kept them. The next question couldn't be answered until now as to what to do with the sermons.

Led by the Holy Spirit and through the Grace of God and my trust in Jesus Christ, this book is the first of a series gathering reflections of the homilies Monsignor Jim shared through his preaching. This book is written out of love and a desire to share his wisdom. The driving force perhaps is my own desire to evangelize, as all Christians have been called to do, by helping others to meet Christ more deeply, trust in Him more fully, or follow Him more faithfully. If this book does that for one person, then this labor of love will have served its purpose.

Monsignor Jim lived as a model of humility, always prayerful, filled with kindness, joy, gentleness, humor, often demonstrating those talents as he sang a few familiar songs or danced with the single ladies in the parish hall of St. Henry's Catholic Church in Pompano Beach, Florida, formerly known as Henry's Hideaway. The parish hall is now dedicated to his name.

This first book in the series is based upon the Resurrection of Christ and the Easter season. Monsignor Jim revealed that Easter Sunday was not just any ordinary Springtime, Chocolate Bunny, or Easter Egg Hunt family fun day! He espoused the annual celebration of the Resurrection of Christ as transformative and easy to be seen in our daily life. What is relevant to you in his messages is that the celebration of the Resurrection reflects Christ living Now and what that means to your life. He believed it was worth living for, staking one's life upon, and trusting even unto death.

Modeling Christ, Monsignor Jim often used stories to highlight gospel passages and bring the gospel messages into contemporary situations. Sometimes a joke or two was inserted just to check if people were awake and listening.

This book and each later book will have twelve chapters. Twelve being a significant biblical number as in the twelve tribes of Israel, the twelve apostles, twelve wicker baskets, twelve stars crowning Mary, twelve days of Christmas, twelve months of the year et cetera. Thus, for this book there are twelve selected sermons dedicated to the Resurrection. You are encouraged to pause between chapters to reflect on the sermon and what may/may not be relevant to you. The chapters do not need to be read consecutively. They are stand-alone writings.

The sermons included here were selected based on my preference. Their messages relate to the Resurrection and its relevance to living a joyous life. There are well over 1000 sermons on various scriptural readings throughout seventy years of Monsignor Jim's preaching. I have tried to associate the readings upon which the sermon was given within the liturgical calendar year and are referenced at the beginning of the sermon. For a better understanding of the sermon, you may want to read the scripture reference on your own. Where possible I have inserted a date, the first, second and Gospel reading reference associated with the sermon and a relevant quote from the scripture.

The reference to the YEAR A, B, or C refers to the Sunday cycle of scriptural readings from the Roman Catholic Church Lectionary from the New Testament. Year A are the Gospel readings mostly from the Gospel of Matthew. Year B, the Gospel readings are from Mark, and chapter 6 of the Gospel of John. Year C is the Gospel readings of Luke. However, the Gospel Readings for Easter season are from the Gospel of John in all three years. The year of the cycle changes on the first Sunday of Advent which is the traditional start of the new liturgical year.

While planning to write this book, I was asked who my target audience is. Hopefully, this book is written for anyone - believer or skeptic, seeker, or servant- who is open to encounter Christ more deeply.

You might want to skip to the end of this book and read the AFTERWORD before reading the contents to get a flavor for who my uncle was as a young man, where he came from, growing up, and how he was active in performing his priestly duties. You will learn about his "experiment in community."

Some of the "Stories" that are contained in Monsignor's sermons were obtained from so many sources over the years it is nearly impossible to track them all. Nor can one say that the stories were themselves passed down through the ages by word of mouth and eventually captured in writing by someone else, then used by Monsignor Jim and here in this book. I did use a plagiarism tracker and apologize in advance to any person who may have 'created' an original story that Monsignor Jim may have used in a homily.

It is not the intent of this book or any future book to deny those sources. Where sources are known, they are acknowledged. Where they are not, the intent has never been ownership but faithful transmission of his written sermon. However, it is Monsignor's message to his various parishioners and to you the reader within the use of the stories that is shared here that I wish to impart.

These homilies were preached not as abstract theology, but as truth - truth that Monsignor Jim lived by and professed.

I invite you now to enter these homilies not as historical artifacts, but as living words-spoken once to parishioners, and now offered anew to you.

With Gratitude,

Kathleen M. Hackett

Ponte Vedra Beach, Florida 2026

Chapter One

SING YOUR HEART OUT

On Easter Sunday April 19, 1981, a short month after the birth of my first born son Matthew (March 16, 1981), Monsignor Reynolds preached the following sermon. The readings for that day were (ACTS 10:34, 37-43; COLOSSIANS 3: 1-4; JOHN 20:1-9) (YEAR A).

"The Lord Has Been Taken From The Tomb!" (John 20:2)

A man we shall call George was accustomed to driving his wife, Rosie, to Church every Sunday. George and Rosie had been married for forty years and they loved each other deeply. They did everything together. They were inseparable in practically every area of their life-except one. When George drove his wife to Church on Sunday, Rosie went in and George remained in the car, reading his newspaper. Rosie died, and for many Sundays thereafter, Church members looked wistfully at the parking lot because George's car was no longer seen there. Several months later, on Easter Sunday, George's car again appeared, and George went into the Church. The preacher delivered a stirring Resurrection sermon and then, as was his custom, invited the members of the congregation to respond. Whereupon, George stood up and, with deep emotion, said firmly, "Rosie lives!" Then he began to sing: "My wild Irish Rose, the sweetest flower that grows ... " One person joined in, then another, and another. Finally, everyone present was joyfully singing what someone later described as "The most beautiful Easter hymn ever sung in our Church."

An enterprising woman decided to cash in on the tradition of singing in the shower. She reasoned that although millions of people sing in the shower, they sometimes forget the lyrics to the song they are singing. Consequently, she designed a series of plastic song sheets on which she printed the words to many song standards. She also fashioned a rubber suction cup with a peg attached. The idea was to attach the suction cup to the shower wall, hang one of the waterproof song sheets on the peg, turn the water on the faucet, and SING YOUR HEART OUT.

> The message of Easter is joy and hope. A victory by Christ over sin & death.
>
> The Lord is Risen, Alleluia! Sing your heart out!
>
> The Lord has won the victory over death! Sing your heart out!
>
> The Lord will come again in glory! Sing your heart out!
>
> The Lord is Risen! Sing your heart out!

From our Sacred Scripture Reading: "It was early in the morning on the first day of the week while it was still dark, Mary Magdalene came to the tomb. She saw that the stone had been moved away, so she ran off to Simon Peter and the other disciples and told them, 'The Lord has been taken from the tomb! We don't know where they have put Him'."

Mary Magdalene's words have been echoing through this world for over 2000 years. Are they not often on our own lips? "We don't know where they have put Him!" We find

Him elusive, this Jesus. Whenever we think we have Him neatly corralled in our private little worlds, we lose Him: "Where have they put Him?"

The answer is: Christ is found in others.

A Maryknoll missionary priest, returning home after 16 years in various mission fields, gives us this answer: "I saw Him in starving people fighting off vultures in Latin America. I saw Him in starving mothers with starving children strapped to their backs in India. I saw Him in 250,000 people sleeping in the streets at night in Calcutta. Working in the midst of all this hunger and pain and indigence, I came to have a new vision of the world. I never saw so many Christs in my life. He is in them by their sufferings."

In another story: According to an ancient tale, Saint Francis of Assisi is riding on horseback through the countryside. He sees a poor leper by the side of the road holding out his wooden bowl, begging. The leper's grotesque features jar St. Francis' sensibilities and he recoils in horror. Then, recovering from the shock, he tosses some coins at the man and gallops away. Soon, however, Francis slackens the pace. He seems unsure of his direction now. Then, he wheels the horse around and gallops back to the leper's station where he jumps to the ground and lovingly embraces him.

"Come," Jesus bids us. "You have My Father's blessing! Inherit the kingdom prepared for you from the creation of the world. For I was hungry and you gave Me food, I was thirsty and you gave Me drink. I was a stranger and you welcomed Me, naked and you clothed Me." To which we reply, "Lord, when did we see you hungry and feed You, or thirsty and give You drink, or naked and clothe You?" Jesus answers, "I assure you as often as you did it for one of My least brothers, you did it for Me." We've heard all this before many times. Then why do we still echo the words of Mary Magdalene? Why do we yet cry out, "The Lord has been taken from us. We don't know where they've put Him. We don't know how to find Him."

Do we entertain the guarded hope that Our Lord will someday absent Himself from the least of our brothers and sisters; that we will discover Him in some tidier package?

During the French Revolution it was fashionable for the intellectuals to start a new religion and introduce it to the people. After having worked out the details a young author approached Monsieur Barreaux, a government official seeking a convincing way to introduce his new religion so that the people would have faith in his teachings. "Well," counseled Barreaux, "I think the best way to prove the worth of what you are saying is to have yourself killed for it and then rise on the third day." Monsieur Barreaux was right. This is the most convincing way to establish a new religion. It's what Christ did.

It's what we are celebrating today-the feast of the Resurrection! And Christ gave us the key to his new religion at the Last Supper: "A new commandment I give to you. That you love one another as I have loved you." He demonstrated this commandment of love by His life of service to others, even unto death so that we could share in the glory of His resurrection and live on in His love.

In today's liturgy for Easter Sunday, Good Friday stands behind us. Let us join with Christ and with one another in celebrating the

Resurrection. Let His love penetrate those things in our lives which deaden our spirits so that we too can share His glory and live on in His love.

Are you ready to SING YOUR HEART OUT that Jesus Christ is Risen?

Chapter Two

OUR REDEEMER LIVES

On Easter Sunday APRIL 22, 1984, just before the birth of my second son, Peter (May 27,1984) Monsignor Reynolds preached the following sermon. The readings for that day were (ACTS 10:34, 37-43; COLOSSIANS 3:1-4; JOHN 20:1-9) (YEAR A).

"They both ran, but the other disciple outran Peter and reached the tomb first." (John 20:4)

There was a crotchety old man who lived with his wife in the backwoods. One day the old mountaineer fell and struck his head against a rock. When his wife found him, he appeared to be quite dead. This happened at a time before morticians would venture up into those hills and so there was no embalming. The "widow" merely summoned a few neighbors to help her dress the body, put it in a plain box, and take it to the place of burial.

As the dead man was being carried from the house by four neighbors, one of them stumbled, causing the coffin to crash into a gatepost. The crash somehow revived the old man. He knocked the cover off the coffin, screamed at everyone, and raised a terrible fuss. One year later, the old man fell sick and died again. Once more the body was placed in the box, and as the pallbearers hoisted their burden and began moving from the house to the burial ground, the widow said firmly, "Watch Out for that gatepost!." Obviously, one resurrection was enough for that long suffering widow.

And so it was for the Apostle Peter. One Resurrection was enough. "Blessed be the God and Father of Our Lord Jesus Christ!" he wrote. "By His great mercy we have been born anew to a living hope through the Resurrection of Jesus Christ from the dead. In this you rejoice, though now for a little while you may have to suffer various trials so that the genuineness of your faith, more precious than gold, may redound to praise and glory and honor at the revelation of Jesus Christ. Without having seen Him, you love Him; though you do not see Him now, you believe in Him. As the outcome of your faith, you obtain the salvation of your soul. (1 Peter 1:3, 6-9)."

Writing in this way, Peter and the other New Testament authors were not merely expressing their views. They were spreading the News: The "Good News" of a God who loves us so much He is always working through His Resurrection Power to give us New Life. The Good News of a God who transforms defeat into victory; despair into hope; sorrow into joy; death into life. This Good News transformed a little band of frightened disciples into flaming evangelists. It was not just the awesome miracle that inspired them. It was the realization that through this miracle, God had revealed to them, as never before, who He is.

We are here to celebrate the Good News of Easter as it is happening NOW! We are here to rejoice together in the presence of the Risen, Living Christ, NOW. We are here to celebrate the Good News that Death's Terror no longer can intimidate or defeat those who live in the Lord by faith. We are here to celebrate the Good News that the God who raised Jesus from the dead will raise also from the defeats of history every word and work and thought offered in obedience to Him who teaches us that to love is to live.

Anton Reicha, the great conductor, was rehearsing his choir for a performance of "The Messiah." The chorus had sung through to the point where the soprano takes up the refrain "I know that my Redeemer Lives." The soloist's technique was perfect, faultless breathing, accurate phrasing, splendid enunciation. When the final note died away, all eyes turned toward Reicha for his approval. But the conductor only looked at the soloist, and with sorrowful eyes, he said "My dear, you do not really believe that your Redeemer lives, do you? The singer nervously replied, "Why, Yes, I think I do." "Then SING IT," cried the conductor, "Sing it so that all who hear you may feel the power and the joy of it!"

The mood in today's Gospel lesson is one of extreme urgency. Mary Magdalene didn't wait even until daybreak to do to Jesus' tomb. She hurried there "while it was still dark." When she saw the empty tomb, she ran to where the

Apostles Peter and John were hiding and told them the news and they ran toward the tomb. ("John outran Peter and got there first.") They desperately needed to know what had happened to Jesus, and when they learned the truth, it made all the difference in their lives.

Most of us didn't come running here today. But we desperately need to know what is happening NOW. As a result of the empty tomb, do we know that Our Redeemer Lives? Can we sing it so that all who hear us may feel the power and the joy of it?

When the Risen Christ appeared to His closest disciples He offered them His gift of Peace. "Peace be with you," He said to them. "As the Father has sent Me, even so I send you." (John 20:21) The Prince of Peace is in our midst NOW. His words are meant directly for us NOW we citizens of the nuclear world. And His tone is urgent. It may be that if and when the holocaust comes, those of us who are getting on in years will be gone. But think about our children and what we are leaving them.

If truly we know that Our Redeemer Lives, we must act upon it so that all who observe us may feel the power of Him who teaches us that to Love is to Live.

The New Testament Christians did not say in dismay "Look what the world has come to!" Rather, they said in delight "Look what has come to the world!"

Today we rejoice over the simple fact that when the disciples when to the tomb they found that it was empty. But our celebration does not end there. Easter is not only something that happened then, but something that happens NOW. Unless it happens NOW to you, then you've missed the point of our celebration. God acted then to confirm the life and ministry of Christ through His Resurrection. God is acting NOW to confirm our life and ministry. God is acting NOW to give us new life, new hope, new expectations. This is what Easter is all about. We don't sit here and remember some dim historical event of the past, we experience it NOW.

Easter is a time to call forth the conviction deep within us that God is in charge, and God is good, and God will take care of us in life and in death. Whatever your present source of deep hurting may be-a personal habit, a broken relationship, the reality of physical death-Easter is NOW!

Despite the din and clamor of this present age, we will hear the calm, confident, reassuring, loving voice of Jesus inviting us into the mystery of faith. "Do you love Me?" Jesus asks over and over. He asks "Do you love Me?" Then "If you love Me, feed my lambs, feed my sheep." The mystery of faith is perfected in love. Jesus invites us to perfect our faith by touching His wounds which lay open before us on the persons of our brothers and sisters. "Blest are they who have not seen and have believed."

There are people everywhere desperately searching for something better in life. We know that their Redeemer lives. The question is "Will they see Him living in us?" The answer is "Not until we see Him living in them!"

"I know that my Redeemer lives; what joy the blest assurance gives, He lives, and grants me daily breath; He lives, and I shall conquer death, He lives, my hungry soul to feed; He lives, to help in time of need, what joy the blest assurance gives. I know that my Redeemer lives!"

Chapter Three

MORE THAN WISHFUL THINKING

On the Second Sunday of Easter APRIL 26, 1981, Monsignor Reynolds preached the following sermon. The readings for that day were (ACTS 2:42-47; 1 PETER 1:3-9; JOHN 20:19-31) (YEAR A).

"Then He breathed on them and said 'Receive the Holy Spirit'" (JOHN 20:22)

There is an old Japanese legend about a man named Seko. When he was a child, Seko was fascinated by stories his parents told him about dragons. As he grew up, dragons became his major preoccupation. At first, he collected stories and images of dragons as a hobby. Then they became his vocation. He was an artist and he devoted most of his time to painting pictures of dragons. His art made him famous, and he became known as "The Dragon Man." He loved dragons. According to the legend, a real live dragon heard about

Seko. The dragon said to himself, "If Seko loves painting dragons so much, he will love me, a real live dragon even more!" So, the dragon went to Seko's studio and stuck his head through the open window. Of course, the artist fled in sheer terror. His love of painting dragons had in no way prepared him for an encounter with a living dragon. So it is that our love for familiar, friendly idols, close to home, in no way prepares us for an encounter with the Holy Spirit of God.

In today's Gospel lesson, Jesus, after His Resurrection, suddenly, miraculously, appears to His disciples. They had hidden themselves away seeking refuge from the religious leaders who had delivered Jesus to His executioners. Jesus stands before them and says "Peace be with you, My Peace be with you. As the Father sent me, so I send you." Then He breathed on them and said, "Receive the Holy Spirit…" (John 20:21-22).

During His entire public ministry, Jesus had been preparing His disciples for that moment. In the Acts of the Apostles, Luke reveals how well Jesus had prepared them to receive the Holy Spirit who would give them light and strength for their Christian ministry: "They sold their goods and possessions and shared out the proceeds…according to what each one needed. They shared their food gladly and generously; they praised God and were looked up to by everyone" (Acts 2:46-47). The Holy Spirit having permeated their lives, they lived accordingly.

Late one December, an elementary school principal said to his teachers: "Let's all write out our new year resolutions about how we can be better teachers and I'll put them on the staff bulletin board. In that way, we can be mutually supportive in our efforts to keep those resolutions." The teachers agreed, and when the resolutions were posted, they all crowded around the bulletin board to read them. One of the young teachers in the group suddenly went into a fit of anger, she said "He didn't put up my resolution, it was one of the first ones in, he doesn't care about me, that just shows what it's like around here." On and on she ranted and raved. The principal, who overheard this from his office, was mortified. He hadn't meant to exclude her resolution. Quickly rummaging through the papers on his desk, he found it and immediately went to the bulletin board and tacked it up. The resolution read "I resolve not to let little things upset me anymore." Resolution, but no commitment!

It takes more than an external show of piety to realize the true presence of the Holy Spirit within us. Like love and marriage there is a necessary ingredient called commitment. Jesus sends the Holy Spirit to reinforce, strengthen, and enlighten our commitment to His ministry, our commitment to His Way of Life, "You are the salt of the earth" Jesus says to His true Disciples. The true followers of Jesus are commissioned to enliven the human condition with a certain flavor. This is the Christian commitment. But when the commitment is weak, when Christians are no longer different from the world they were commissioned to change, the salt loses its flavor. Christians are called not merely to proclaim Jesus' solution to the world's ills, they must be part of the solution.

Saint Paul has written "Far from relying on any power of my own, I came among you in great fear and trembling, and in my speeches and sermons that I gave there were none of the arguments that belong to philosophy; only a demonstration of the power of the Spirit" (1 Cor. 2:3-4). It is not enough for Christians to say they have received the Holy Spirit, they must demonstrate it. For Jesus's followers this means a commitment to life entirely within the context of the rule of God: Citizenship, if you will, in God's Kingdom in which patriotism is not demonstrated in an occasional, pious, emotional outburst, but in the steadfast dedication of a lifetime.

In a shopping mall, a married couple stopped at a wishing well standing in the center of the arcade. The wife playfully tossed in a coin, for a moment, the husband looked wistfully into the fountain, then threw in his coin. "What did you wish for?" the wife asked. "I just wished that I could afford whatever it was you wished for" the husband replied.

The gift of the Holy Spirit does not come as the result of our wishful thinking.

The gift is tendered always. God never withdraws His Love, His offer of Grace. But acceptance to realize the gift, to accept the gift we must be ready, willing, and able to say "Yes, Lord! I want to live under your rule. I will wholeheartedly embrace your plan for my fulfillment."

"Receive the Holy Spirit." God is offering to bring something new into your life. If you should ask, "what is one-half of eight," the answer would come "four." But the figure of eight (8) is made up of two zeros. Take away one zero and one half of eight is zero. Now draw a vertical line down the center of the 8 and you will have two threes face-to face. By seeing things differently, we can make new discoveries. We can get a new slant of old hangups. We can see old ideas in a new light and all because we were willing to let into our life something that did not exist before. Open up your heart and mind and will to the possibility of God bringing into your life something that did not exist before: "Receive the Holy Spirit," answer the call to Jesus' new life with a resounding "Yes, Lord." Commit your life to the rule of God. Accept Jesus' commission to go out into the world in the spirit of loving service. Do this and you will experience at the deepest level of your being, the peace that the world can not give: the peace of Christ.

Francis Bacon (an English philosopher) once said: "It is not what we eat but what we digest that makes us strong; Not what we gain but what we save that makes us rich; Not what we read but what we remember that makes us learned; Not what we preach but what we practice that makes us Christian."

Strengthened and enlightened by the gift of the Holy Spirit, we can, we will, practice what we preach.

The God of Israel spoke these words to His people: "I am the Lord, Your God, who brought you out of the land of Egypt, out of the house of bondage." In that sentence is summarized the great promise. The greatest theme in scripture from beginning to end: That Almighty God, the God who has created the heavens and the earth, the God who has given you life, loves you. He is a gracious God who called Israel and has been calling His people ever since out of slavery, out of bondage, into freedom, into the land of promise. Our deep longing for fulfillment is more than wishful thinking.

"Receive the Holy Spirit!"

Chapter Four

DO MEN DIE FOR A LIE?

This sermon has no date. I do not know if Monsignor actually preached this message. It was found in his files for the Third Sunday of Easter (Year B), and it inspired the title of this book.

"Have you any food to eat? (from Luke 24:13-35)

The most important event in all history is the one we celebrate at Easter time for without the Resurrection, we couldn't be sure that Christ was the Messiah. Without the Resurrection, we couldn't be sure that Christ was the "Son of God." Without the Resurrection, we couldn't be sure that Christ was the true Redeemer.

Saint Paul said, "If Christ be not risen, then our preaching is in vain and vain is your faith." (1 Corinthians 15:12-19). His Resurrection is the cornerstone of our faith. Do Men Die for a Lie?

We could ask Mary Magdalene, Mary His Mother, or Apostle Thomas. But let's let a few years pass by and ask Peter at his crucifixion on a cross - then Paul before his beheading in Rome-then the other Apostles. Do men die for a lie?

Just before the turn of the century, a train rumbled through a French province of Normandy headed for Paris. Two men sat opposite each other: the one a young soldier obviously bored with the inactivity, the other an old man quite content to quietly finger his rosary beads. As the monotonous miles bumped along, the soldier could restrain himself no longer. He blurted out in the direction of the old man: "God isn't going to save our world, science is!" The old man merely smiled and nodded, continuing to move the next bead through his fingers. The "put down" was too much of a challenge to avoid, so the young man launched into a tirade on the marvels of science in business and medicine. Declaring religion to be dying out as the light of science came in, he continued his attack until the train came into the Paris depot. As the youth stood up to get his bag, he felt sorry for the old man silently taking the abuse for the past hour. Trying to sound a bit kinder, he introduced himself. The ancient one shook the soldier's hand and reached into his vest for a card. The youngster accepted the card and helped the old man down the step. Then he glanced at the card: "Dr. Louis Pasteur, Academy of Science, Paris."

All of us are surprised when the least expected person turns out to be the expert and produces the right answers.

An inmate behind the fence of the mental institution watched a man outside standing by his car, after kids had run off with the bolts to one of his tires. "Take one bolt from each of the other tires and use them to hold that one until you get to a gas station" the inmate said. "That's a fine idea. What are you doing in there?" "Well, I may be insane, but I'm not stupid." The same with us. We just don't have faith in certain people. We sell them short.

The disciples on the road to Emmaus couldn't see Christ because they were convinced, he was still dead. Mary Magdalene was the same. She couldn't see Christ in the garden because she didn't look through the eyes of faith: faith in the Risen Lord. Thomas, the Apostle, was also in denial.

And in today Gospel lesson, (Luke 24) the Disciples were terribly disturbed by a "ghost" because they were convinced Christ had died for good. In a very human way, Christ asked them if they had anything to eat. Ghosts usually don't behave that way. Legend has it that the famous ghost, Count Dracula, would only be interested in blood, not something to eat.

The same applies even more to our vision of Christ. If we only have faith in a remote god-creator who somehow keeps the world going, then we will not see and experience the God-man Christ who knows our problems, walks with us, accepts us for the way we are. We won't grow. We won't know what a Pentecostal is talking about. To "experience" the divine presence of Jesus is just too emotional for us. If Jesus Christ asked for a bite of our fish - he couldn't be God. He is too common, too available.

But there's always some doubt on our part. As Saint Peter suggests, we can "put to death the author of life" by our ignorance. If we don't have faith in the Risen, loving Lord - He's as good as dead for us.

Let Easter time increase our Faith. Have the right faith-vision of Christ. Saint John writes: "The way we can be sure of our knowledge of Him is to keep His commandments. Love others as I have loved you." At rock bottom this means appreciating those we think little of - "When is the last time you seriously listened to a "little kid?" Then we should start "acting" like Christ is right alongside of us. Talk to Him during the day and share events. If we really get good at this practice, soon the reality will dawn on us. The "Power of Christ" will move us with sheer joy and wonder. And we will begin to know that "God raised Him from the dead, and we are His witnesses." Then the peace and joy of the Apostles will be ours. And we will want to spread the Good News. Maybe even begin today when you turn to the one next to you and proclaim:

"The Lord is Risen, peace be with you."

Chapter Five

EVERY DAY A LITTLE BIT

On the third Sunday of Easter APRIL 9, 1978, Monsignor Reynolds preached the following sermon. The readings for that day were (ACTS 2:14, 22-28; 1 PETER 17-21; LUKE 24:13-35) (YEAR B).

"What little sense you have! How slow you are to believe all that the prophets have announced! Did not the Messiah have to undergo all this so as to enter into His glory?" (Luke 24:25-26)

Several years ago, an international poll was taken to discover the name of the person most widely recognized throughout the whole world. The result was surprising to many people. The most widely recognized person was not the President of the United States, nor the Pope in Rome, nor the heavy weight boxing champion Mohamed Ali. It was a soccer player from Brazil, a man named Pele. He is so well known internationally, first of all, because no less than 140 countries take part in the world cup soccer matches and secondly, he was such a great player, he was able to lead his team from Brazil to an unprecedented three world cup championships. But there is a third reason for his worldwide popularity: He is a good man. People respect and love him as a good man. He recently played his last game. There were 75,000 people in the stadium, millions more watching on TV. Pele stood in the center of the arena during a moment of final tribute to him as a player and said to the crowd, "Say after me, three times, Love, Love, Love." Each time he said the word Love the people thundered back, "LOVE!" Then he made a little closing speech in English, a language he had learned only three years earlier. He said "This moment is very unhappy, I stop to do what I like to do most in life: play soccer." Then he added softly, "I die a little bit today."

Because, in one way or another, all of us have been there before. We can identify with Pele in that situation. "I die a little bit today." That is a direct reflection of words Saint Paul wrote to his friends in the Corinthian Church. "I die every day, a little bit" he said. Paul's experience of the living Christ had so transformed his life that he set out on a lifelong mission in the Mediterranean world to share this experience with others, and, literally, he died a little bit every day, as he explained to the people of Corinth: "Five times," Paul said, "I received forty lashes less one; three times I was beaten with rods; I was stoned once; shipwrecked three times; I traveled continually, endangered by floods, robbers, my own people, the gentiles, imperiled in the city, in the desert, at sea, by false brothers; enduring labor, hardship, many sleepless nights; in hunger and thirst and frequent fastings; in cold and nakedness, leaving other sufferings unmentioned, there is that daily tension pressing on me, my anxiety for all the churches" (2 Corinthians 11:24-28) It leaves one Breathless!

It is a striking thing to notice that in First Corinthians Paul speaks of his daily deaths in the context of a powerful discourse on the Resurrection with great clarity he is saying that the God of Resurrection Power is always working in our lives through a process of death and Resurrection. Unless there is the death of the grain of seed, there can be no new life, no harvest. Resurrection is the new Life, the new thing that God does for us. But it must come through death. It is the way God works in His universe. Paul, therefore, is telling us to first learn what Resurrection means to us in our daily dying so that, when the time comes for our bodily death, we will be so caught up in the Resurrection Spirit, it will be for us a moment of Glory!

Every day we die a little bit. A newborn baby gives up the comfort and warmth of the mother's womb in order to have life. A child gives up the security of home life in order to start school. A student gives up the comfort of the structured academic life in order to graduate. A young man or woman gives up the accustomed family life in order to marry. The daily deaths come in countless other ways too: Broken relationships, illness, divorce, death of a loved one. A man counts his daily deaths by the number of times he gets up in the morning to go to a job he hates. Another's daily death is not to be able to find work at all.

Here is the story of a seminary instructor who was lecturing a class of future preachers. He was trying to impress upon the students the importance of using facial expressions to express their feelings when preaching. "When you speak of Heaven" he said, "Let your face light up and be irradiated with a heavenly gleam, let your eyes shine with reflective glory. When you speak of Hell, your everyday face will have to do."

There is a time when your everyday face and my everyday face reflect the Hell we are going through. Saint Paul, out of his knowledge and experience of Jesus Christ, tells us it is at that very moment that God's Resurrection Power is working in our lives; that God is bringing life out of that death; that God is bringing life out of that pain and suffering; that God is bringing life out of that loss.

It's all there in the lines of the old spiritual someone has called, "the greatest poem ever written in America." "Nobody knows the trouble I've seen, Nobody knows my sorrow. Nobody knows the trouble I've seen, Glory Hallelujah!" Nobody knows the trouble I've seen, but Glory Hallelujah, God is God! God is a God of Resurrection Power.

In todays' Gospel lesson, two of the disciples encounter the Risen Jesus as they walk toward the village of Emmaus. They do not recognize Him, however, and they proceed to tell Him the whole story about the Crucifixion and the empty tomb. They are confused and distressed, "We were hoping that He was the one who would set Israel free" they said to Jesus, when they had finished reciting their story. Then Jesus says to them, "What little sense you have! How slow you are to believe all that the prophets have announced. Did not the Messiah have to undergo all this so as to enter into His Glory?" (Luke 24:25-27). Jesus left the comfort of Mary's womb and was delivered into a cold barn in order that He might have life. From that moment on, He became subject to the way God works, the process of Death/Resurrection, day by day. And when the agony of Gethsemane was upon Him, He was prepared for it. "Not My will be done, but Yours," He prayed to the Father, whereupon, He emptied himself, gave up everything and died to the world in order to receive His Glory. Did you not know that the Messiah had to undergo all this so as to enter into His glory?

Not long ago, a Washington, D.C. newspaper announced that Betty Grant was going to retire. Years earlier, she had been stricken with polio. She could talk, see, and hear, and had the use of her toes, but the rest of her body was totally paralyzed. She had a daughter to raise. Talk about dying daily! Lying in bed day after day, concerned about her life, concerned about her future, concerned about her daughter's future, she thought "Well, I'll make use of what I have." She contacted the telephone company, and they rigged up a switchboard she could work with her toes, and she started a 24 hour a day answering service. For 16 years she continued this business and supported her daughter through college. Interviewed on the occasions of her retirement, Betty Grant's closing words were "God has been so good to me!"

"Did not the Messiah have to undergo death to enter into His glory?"

We will never know how good God has been to us until we learn to accept the way in which He is working through us for our fulfillment. Every day we die a little bit so that at the moment of final, physical death - we may enter into our glory by the Resurrection Power of God in Jesus Christ.

The seed you sow does not germinate unless it dies.

Chapter Six

ARE YOU LISTENING?

On the 4th Sunday of Easter May 13, 1984, Monsignor Reynolds preached the following sermon. The readings for that day were (ACTS 2:14, 36-41; 1 PETER 2:20-25; JOHN 10:1-10) (YEAR A).

"The sheep hear His voice as He calls His own by name and leads them out." (JOHN 10:3)

It was high noon in midtown Manhattan, the streets were buzzing with activity: crowds of people scurrying to lunch; auto horns honking; breaks screeching; a siren wailing. Two men were making their way together through the throng, one was a native New Yorker, the other a Kansas farmer on a visit. Suddenly, the farmer stopped and said to the city dweller, "Hold on! I hear a cricket." His friend replied, "Are you kidding? Even if there were a cricket around here, which isn't likely, you would never be able to hear it over all this noise." The farmer remained quiet for a few moments, then walked several paces to the corner where a bush was growing in a large cement planter. He turned several leaves over and found the cricket. The city man was flabbergasted, "What great ears you have," he said. "No," the farmer replied, "your ears are as good as mine, it's a matter of what you've been conditioned to listen for, I'll show you." Whereupon, he pulled a handful of coins from his pocket and let them drop to the sidewalk, as if on signal, every head on the block turned. "You see," said the farmer, you hear what you want to hear. It's a matter of what you're listening for."

In today's Gospel reading, Jesus teaches this same lesson. Using the imagery of a shepherd and his flock. In Jesus' time (and even today in the area of the Holy Land), the shepherds brought their flocks back from the fields at night and herded them together in a common enclosure. In the morning, the shepherds would return to the big pen and each in turn would call out to his own sheep to follow him. Remarkably, the sheep would sort themselves out by flock in response to their particular shepherd's voice. There was no confusion about this, each sheep would wait to hear its own shepherd's voice before moving out. For the nourishment and guidance and care required to sustain its life, each sheep recognized the voice of its one, true shepherd.

"I am the Good Shepherd," Jesus said, for the nourishment and guidance and care you need to enrich your life to the fullest, "Follow Me!" He said. "Take up your Cross daily and follow Me," He said.

It is not possible for you to hear the Good Shepherd's Voice on Sunday and the voices of other shepherds during the rest of the week, it won't work! "You cannot serve two masters…you can not serve both God and Mammon."

Jesus warned His would-be followers again and again. The voice of the Good Shepherd and the voices of the world are in conflict. You must choose between them. Either you "will hate the one and love the other or be attentive to one and despise the other." (Luke 6:13)

In our time as in no other, multi-million-dollar campaigns bring the voice of mammon directly into our homes seven days a week. "Listen! You can have the good life" we are told, "if only you will buy this or that, wear this or that, eat this or that, drink this or that." To give one example, there have been enormous TV Commercial campaigns aimed at encouraging young people to drink more beer. Most of the actors used in the commercials appear to be in their early twenties and the message is that the key to real happiness is guzzling beer. To quote the punch line from one of the big campaigns "It doesn't get any better than this!" Meanwhile, there is another voice (could it be the voice of God?) telling us about the grim statistics on drunk-driving episodes in which tens of thousands of human beings are being killed and crippled each year.

Jesus warns us: stop worrying over questions like, "What are we to eat, or what are we to drink, or what are we to wear? The unbelievers are always running after these things. Your heavenly Father knows all that you need. Seek first His Kingship over you,

His way of holiness, and all these things will be given to you besides." (Matthew 6:31-33).

It is a matter of priorities. It is a matter of putting "first things first." Last night it might have been a matter of being more concerned with being a safe driver than with satisfying your thirst for alcohol. Earlier today, it might have been a matter of being more concerned with what you were going to do here than with what you were going to wear. Later today, and through the week, it might be a matter of being more concerned with what you are going to give than with what your are going to get. It might be a matter of being more concerned with what you can share than with what you can take. It might be a matter of being more concerned with "things as they ought to be" than with "things as they are." It might be a matter of being more concerned with "doing it God's way" than "doing it your way."

A young man was faced with making an important decision that would affect the course of his life. He considered his grandmother to be the wisest person he knew, and so he went to see her. "Grandmother," he said, "I need to make the right decision about my life and I've prayed about it, but I just can't decide. Nothing happens when I pray, tell me please, how can I hear the voice of God?" The grandmother thought for a while, then replied, "My dear grandson, I have quite a different problem and because of it, I don't think I can help you. You see I can not hear the voice of God."

You hear what you want to hear. You hear what your are listening for. If you want to hear the voice of God, you can not hear it. God never gives up on you. God never stops inviting you to be His own. The Good Shepherd always keeps you within calling distance. If you don't hear Him, it's not because He is too far away or He's not speaking loudly enough. It's because you are listening for other voices.

Week after week we come together and some men named Matthew, Mark, Luke, John, and Paul try to tell us that the word became flesh and entered into time and yet walked within the boundaries of an eternal rhythm.

Are You Listening?

They try to tell us of the LOVE that was beyond measure.

Are You Listening?

They try to tell us of a hope beyond reason.

Are You Listening?

They try to tell us of the abundant life being offered to all who walk within the boundaries of the eternal rhythm.

Are You Listening?

They try to tell us that only when we are walking within the boundaries of the eternal rhythm can we begin to experience the peace and joy and love we need and want for our life's fulfillment.

Are You Listening?

But little did they know, those New Testament Writers, how busy we would be! Little did they know how important our work would be! Little did they know how time-consuming and soul-consuming our quest for possessions would be!

Little did they know that the mere tinkling of coins could lure us out of the boundaries of the eternal rhythm.

Chapter Seven

THIS TREMENDOUS LOVER

On the 4th Sunday of Easter MAY 6, 1979, Monsignor Reynolds preached the following sermon. The readings for that day were (ACTS 4:3-12; 1 JOHN 3:1-2; JOHN 10:11-18) (Year B).

"I know My Sheep and My Sheep know Me in the same way that the Father knows Me." (JOHN 10:14-1).

The Apostle John summarized the tremendous reality of God's love in a simple phrase, one of the most familiar verses in the Bible. "God is Love." But who can say that he or she has even begun to grasp the implications of that simple, profound truth? Because all else in our faith and life depends on it. We must return to it over and over again, reflect on it, ponder over it, wonder about it, and experience it ever deeper.

Recently some newspapers ran a photograph of a piece of Graffiti someone had painted on the "Department of Languages" building of a large university. It read, "Where will you spend eternity?" Immediately below, someone else had written: "As far as I can see, it looks like German 201." Perhaps, to some of you it seems that we are eternally preaching about the love of God. But if we believe Jesus who tells us that everything in our faith and life depends on experiencing God's love, then how can we not preach this reality in season and out?

Francis Thompson was a man who lived through a severe identity crisis. Although he had not the slightest intention of becoming a doctor, nevertheless, he spent six years of his life preparing for a career in medicine, why? Because his father wanted him to be a doctor, he did it to please his father. Then, after six years, he couldn't stand it anymore. He dropped out of school. He sold encyclopedias. He worked as a clerk in a retail store. Finally, he joined the army but was soon discharged because he was physically unable to be a soldier. Then he started wandering around. As a kind of vagrant, he became a heavy cocaine user. He contracted tuberculosis and died at the age of 48. But just a few years before he died, he had discovered his identity. It was to be a writer. There was a gift within him that he slowly became aware of and then began to share with others. He wrote a poem which has been acclaimed as the greatest ode, or lyric poem, in the English language. It is called "The Hound of Heaven." The poem is a direct commentary on the 139th Psalm and it is a story of Francis Thompson' relationship with God. It is the story of how God had been chasing after him through all those years of knocking around. He has always been running away from God. But God was always in hot pursuit. The "Hound of Heaven" padding after him, relentlessly, lovingly. At one point in the poem, Francis Thompson hauntingly refers to the God who constantly pursued him as "This Tremendous Lover." Only when he turned and allowed himself to be caught by "This Tremendous Lover," was he able to live in a fulfilling way.

"This Tremendous Lover!" Open yourself up to that phrase! Let it come back to haunt you, again and again! Let it remind you that whatever you may say about God, what ever you may think about God, Jesus is telling you that He is "This Tremendous Lover;" that this is who God is. Sometimes He pursues you gently; sometimes He pursues you firmly; but at all times He pursues you lovingly.

Today, bookstores and magazines are crammed with information on living well: how to eat, how to sleep, how to make money, how to make love. But there is no meaning, ultimately, in any of these things until we have allowed ourselves to be caught by "The Hound of Heaven;" until we have allowed the power of "This Tremendous Lover" to make sense out of our eating and sleeping and making money and making love and all the other things that we do in this life. And it is not enough to believe this intellectually, it is knowing with our whole being that it is essential.

When we come to know God as "This Tremendous Lover," we become more and more eager just to be with Him. We become more and more aware of what Jesus is talking about in today's Gospel lesson when He says, "I know my sheep and my sheep know me in the same way the Father knows Me and I know the Father" (John 1: 14-15)

Jesus often withdrew by Himself onto the lake or up into the mountain or out into the wilderness for times of prayer and meditation. He did this partly because He needed it. But more because He wanted it. He was eager to experience the joy He found in communion with "This Tremendous Lover." In recent years, books on prayer and meditation have been pouring out of the religion publication houses. People everywhere are talking about the need in their lives for quiet time, for reflection, for meditation, more and more, people are embarking on that inward journey and writing about the experience. But more often than not, the experience comes off as a heavy, burdensome exercise. A discipline that is not Good News. People struggle with meditation as if it were a stringent diet. They are fighting it, in other words; analyzing it, intellectualizing it. Yet for centuries, our rich tradition of contemplative prayer in the Church has been saying that what prayer is ultimately about is just being with God. Not telling God what we want, not telling God what to do, not telling God how to get through to us, but just being with Him. When we really begin to know how much God loves us, when we begin to know the Father as Jesus knows Him, we will want to be with Him in a prayerful way. We will be eager to be with Him. Prayer will no longer be a burden, but a joy, and we will begin to relate to one another in a whole new way.

We all have needs. We make demands on other people to meet those needs. We do this subconsciously. For example, a mother or father may demand that a child turn out a certain way, not realizing that it is an attempt to satisfy his or her own need, rather than the child's. Or, a benefactor goes out into the community to minister to the poor and returns to announce how ungrateful those people are. Clearly, he had ministered to the poor because of his own need for people to be grateful to him. This manipulative attitude and approach to other people, whether it be conscious or unconscious, is a destructive element in our relationships with others. It can destroy marriages, break up families, alienate societies. But... when you know that God loves you, when you really know that, when you are open to His love at the center of your being, you find that His power and His love are meeting your needs. That is where your needs are met: by the power of the Almighty God, Himself. Take your strength from "This Tremendous Lover" and no longer will you need to make demands on other people. You will be able to be present to them in a whole new way; to love them for their own sake.

The story is told of how Theodore Roosevelt coped with his inability to remember names, a serious problem for any political figure. Whenever he was greeted by an old acquaintance whose name he couldn't remember, Mr. Roosevelt would quickly ask "And how is your old complaint these days?" Immediately, the person would begin talking about his old complaint (everybody had one) and would not notice Roosevelt's failure to greet him by name. (He must have remembered me because he remembered my old complaint).

Try it this week, you'll be amazed at the result. Everybody is afflicted with an "old complaint" and the need to burden someone else with it. We all do it. We try to resolve the "old complaint" by making demands upon other people. But when we are aware of how

God is working on our "old complaint," healing it and bringing new life out of it, then we are free to be present to other people in a life-giving way.

In Alan Paton's book, "Cry the Beloved Country," there is a scene in which a distraught father, who is estranged from his son whom he deeply loves, seeks aid and comfort from his friend, the village priest. The father says to him, "I feel that God has turned away from me," and gently, the village priest replies, "there are times when that may seem to happen, but it never does. Never, never, never does that happen."

There may be times when it seems to us that God has turned away. But I say to you today, by the grace of God, in our Lord Jesus Christ, that never, never, never does that happen. "I know My sheep and my sheep know Me, the same way the Father knows Me." (John 10:14-15). God is "This Tremendous Lover" who is always eager to give us life.

To know the Father in this way is to know Him as Jesus knows Him.

Chapter Eight

ARE WE ALL SUNK?

On the Fifth Sunday of Easter MAY 17, 1981, Monsignor Reynolds preached the following sermon. The readings for that day were (ACTS 6: 1-7; 1 PETER 2:4-9; JOHN 14:1-12) (YEAR A).

"Do not let your hearts be troubled, have faith in God and faith in Me" (JOHN 14: 1)

A young lad always concluded his night prayers with a few supplications. "Dear God," he would say, "please take care of mommy and daddy and baby brother and Aunt Sara, etc." One night, after the day's events had left him with a troubled heart he said "Dear God, please take good care of mommy, daddy, baby brother, grandma, grandpa, Aunt Sara - and please take extra good care of yourself, or we're all sunk!"

In times like ours, it is so easy for us to become bogged down in a mood of despair.

The problems all around us are so great man's inhumanity to man is so shocking that it is easy to see only the bad side of things. It is easy to allow ourselves to get pulled down into a whirlpool of insecurity and cry out despairingly... "We're Sunk!"

In one of their classic recordings, Peter, Paul, and Mary sing out "The times they are A-change-in.'" But often it seems as though we are going from bad to worse as we change. Almost every conversation, no matter where it starts, ends up in this kind of mood.

One is reminded by this of the college student who enrolled in a course entitled "Theology I." The course had become known on campus as a "snap course" because no one ever failed. It seems that year after year the professor always asks the same final examination question. The question was "Discuss the trials and tribulations of Job." The students, knowing what was coming, were well prepared and would have no trouble passing. One year, however, the professor surprised them, he changed the question and only one student passed. The new question was "criticize the Sermon on the Mount." The answer given by the one student who passed began as follows: "Far be it from me to criticize Our Lord! However, there are a few things I would like to say about the trials and tribulations of Job! He then went on to fill up his paper and he passed the course!

That's the way it is these days when we start a conversation on any subject. The weather, the baseball standings, the latest fashions - and end it up on the trials and tribulations of life in today's world, and we are soon caught up in a mood of despair. It is so easy for us to slip into this kind of mood when "the times, they are A-change-in." That is why it is important for us to remind ourselves that the people of God are a people of JOY, because God gives Himself to us even in our darkest situations. And as He gives Himself to us, He gives us JOY.

"Do not let your heart be troubled." Jesus tells us in today's gospel lesson, "Have faith in God and faith in Me… anything you ask Me in My Name I will do" (John 14:1-14).

We are not sunk, nor are we in danger of being sunk. Jesus is telling us, as long as we keep the faith, Jesus and the Father not only take care of themselves, they take care of us.

It is amazing as we look at the record and discover how God's people faced difficult situations in biblical times. They didn't try to escape from reality by pretending things were better than they were. They penetrated more deeply into the life of the world and there they always found their saving God. Because of this, no matter what happened to them, an undercurrent of deep, throbbing joy, always comes through. It comes through from the very beginning: in the story of Abraham, Isaac, and Jacob; in the story of Moses and Miriam singing and dancing for joy in what we call "The Song of Miriam"; in the story of King David dancing in ecstatic joy before the Ark of the Covenant; in the story of the prophet Isaiah, even when the Assyrians were overrunning his little country and threatening to destroy everything he loved, crying out "The desert shall rejoice and blossom like a rose." Then we come to the New Testament, which is a collection of books of joy. The word Gospel itself means Good News, and it begins with "Tidings of great Joy that shall be to all people" and the Gospel ends with the

Disciples coming back to Jerusalem "With Great Joy." From beginning to end, that throbbing undercurrent of Joy constantly breaks through. Nowhere in the New Testament is this exemplified more beautifully than in the writings of Paul. There are probably few people in all human history who know more of individual suffering than Paul did. He was beaten time and again, he was stoned, he was imprisoned, he was shipwrecked, he was ridiculed, he was misunderstood, even by those who loved him most. In addition, all around him were the massive social problems of his time: millions of people living in abject slavery, millions of people hungry, thousands of Christians dying violent deaths simply because they were Christians. Yet, again and again, Paul wrote to his little congregations, "Rejoice in the Lord, Always, Again I will say "Rejoice!"

The New Testament message, as we see it exemplified in Paul, is a message of Joy. Because God is God and there is nothing that man can do that will ultimately defeat God. We live in a world in which the problem of starving millions is still unresolved, the TV News confronts us daily with the problems of unemployment, inflation, terrorism, street crime, assassinations, white-collar crime, family disintegration, political betrayal, drug addiction, to name a few. But in the midst of this we are called not to a withdrawal from the problems and realities of life, but to a deeper penetration into them in order to discover that God is there. God is there as a healing God, as a gracious God, as a redeeming God, who will lead us ultimately into the promised land of our fulfillment.

This is why the New Testament Christians, in their own particular set of trying circumstances could rejoice. This is why on a day like just like this one, they could sing songs of praise and thanksgiving to God and go out into the world as a Joy-Filled People.

A little girl was asked by her Sunday school teacher, "Who made you?" She replied, "To tell you the truth, I'm not done yet." It is very important for us to remind ourselves that "We're not done yet! "The world is not done yet. God's creative order is in the process of becoming. You and I are in the process of becoming the uniquely beautiful, fulfilled persons God created us to be. But God's plan is still unfolding for us. However mysterious it may seem, God's work is not done yet.

An ancient legend tells of a King who was deeply troubled. Weary of life, he withdrew more and more into himself, trying to escape from reality. Finally, members of his family consulted with the official wise man of the Royal Court. "How can we bring Joy back into his life?" they asked. After talking with the King and studying his depression, the wise man announced that if the King would wear a happy person's shirt for one week, his spirits would be renewed, and he would be happy again. Immediately, the Royal Family began to search for a happy person. None could be found at court, so they went out among the people to look again. They searched in vain. Then they came upon a beggar lying under a tree. The man's face bore a look of utter serenity, he seemed totally at peace. "Are you a happy man?" they asked. "Yes," The beggar replied. "My soul is filled with Joy." They asked him if there was anything he needed or wanted. "Oh no" he replied. "I am quite content." Then they told him of their mission and asked if they might have his shirt for the King. At this the beggar laughed heartedly, and as he arose from the dry leaves that covered him said "I have no shirt!."

Even in the darkest situation, even when it seems the whole world has gone crazy, even when you don't have a shirt on your back, Jesus is telling you: "Do not let your hearts be troubled, have faith in God and faith in Me."

Have faith in the God who created you out of love and is inviting you into his Life of Love. Then the deep throbbing undercurrent of Joy that God's people have experienced from the beginning will be yours to cherish - and to share.

Chapter Nine

A PRICELESS GIFT

On the Fifth Sunday of Easter, April 28, 1991, Monsignor Reynolds preached the following sermon. The readings for that day were (ACTS 9:26-31; 1 John 3:18-24; John 15: 1-8) (Year B).

"I am the vine, and you are the branches" (John 15:5)

Theodore Roosevelt is credited with this story about two men who were talking politics. One said to the other, "Why are you a Republican?" The other replied, "because my father was a Republican and before him my grandfather was a Republican." To which the first man replied, "What a stupid, weak-kneed reason! What would you be if your father was a horse thief and your grandfather a bank-robber?" "Then I'd probably be a Democrat" (In retelling the joke, you can change roles as your circumstances call for).

In recent years, large numbers of US voters have detached themselves from the major political parties and have become "Independents." Moreover, a new wave of independence has been intensifying in many areas of modern living. Even in the Church this has happened to some extent. The loyal citizen who switches political parties or detaches from them and becomes an 'Independent' remains a loyal citizen.

For the loyal Christian, however, there is no possibility of switching or detaching or changing labels. There is but one Gospel message: one Spirit, one Lord Jesus Christ, one Father of us all, one God who is love. "I am the Vine," Jesus says in today's Gospel lesson, "and you are the branches."

The loyal Christian cannot be detached from the Vine, cannot be independent of the Vine and remain loyal. The episode in today's lesson occurs on the last night of Jesus' life. As He did on almost every occasion when He was with His disciples, Jesus reminded them that the most important thing in life is to find God and to love Him with all your being. God is always reaching out to offer us life, and it is in being attached to God that we will find life.

Using the image of the Vineyard, this is what Jesus is telling the Disciples in today's Gospel episode. He tells them to picture themselves as the branch that is attached to God, the Vine. As long as they remain attached to the main vine, the very life of the Vine can run through them, and they can produce rich fruit. But if they become detached from the Vine, they will wither and die. If any of you are withering and dying right now in some area of your life, it is because you have become detached from the Vine.

Jesus says, literally, "Apart from Me, you can do nothing!" Apart from Me there is no fruit, no life, no harvest, no fulfillment. That is the opening message of the 15th chapter of John. But Jesus goes on to tell us in a surprising way for some of us how we remain attached to the Vine. He tells us that the way in which we remain attached to God is by loving other persons. Suddenly, we find ourselves confronted once again with this basic teaching of Jesus: If we do not love other people, then we literally block the flow of God's life within us.

In his New Testament letter, John says - "Those who do not love, do not know God!" A sure-fire way to love another person is found throughout the Gospels. Jesus shows us by example that one of the most creative ways we can love the persons who are close to us is simply by listening. Jesus listened carefully to Peter - who never seemed to let up in his religious searching; to James and John, whose enthusiasm sometimes carried them off in wrong directions; to Thomas with his doubts; to Nicodemus who wanted desperately to be able to attach meaning to his life: to the "woman at the well' who needed someone to talk to, someone to take her seriously.

Listening is something many of us do not do very well! Listening is a form of personal contact and people need personal contact these days. Lack of personal contact makes life less interesting.

Sometime ago, two officials from a government employment agency concerned with finding jobs for men released from prison, tried an experiment. One of them pretended he had just been released from jail after 20 yrs. The other acting as an official accompanied him on a visit to the personnel offices of several large companies. The man pretending to be an ex-prisoner reported that not once did the personnel staff speak to him, and mostly they did not even look at him. They directed all their questions about him to the official. Any former convict faces their biggest difficulty in finding employment by getting people to deal with him as a person. As long as the refusal to address a person lasts, there is no possibility of human contact. Keeping in contact is related to the central theme of today's gospel, where Jesus insists on the need to abide in Him, to be in contact with Him.

To consider maintaining contact with Christ, we have to think about the way we keep in contact with others. People need personal contact - The lack of personal contact makes life less interesting. Here are some examples:
1) While shopping in a supermarket have you ever had the misfortune of being served by a clerk who continues a conversation with another clerk while supposedly attending to

your needs - or ringing up the cash register, particularly with prices these days. Some lady remarked: "I always wanted to spend money lavishly, but I didn't think it would be for mayonnaise, bread, and peanut butter." Don't you feel you are not really being treated as a customer should be treated? 2) Have you ever been to a cocktail party and while talking with someone they look over your shoulder apparently looking for someone else? Doesn't it make you feel more like a steppingstone than like a person? 3) If you have a friend who is blind, ask him about the strange widespread reaction of people who meet him for the first time. Rather than speak to him directly, people often direct their words to the sighted person with him, "Will he have cream in his coffee?" 4) A home loses its warmth when parents are not speaking. 5) A good job loses its appeal when the atmosphere at work is strained by co-workers who are not on good speaking terms. 6) A whole neighborhood can be changed by a few neighbors who can't get along.

On the other hand, personal contact adds zest to life. Maybe that is why we like our friends to write, to send a card, to keep in touch.

Contact, even if occasionally, nourishes friendships. Bell Telephone runs TV ads showing how contact is a big help to the student away from home, the elderly parent, the homemaker whose husband is away at a business meeting. "Long distance calls make the heart grow fonder." Of course, they neglect to say that these calls also make the telephone bill grow bigger! Maybe the big attraction of having "a beer with the boys" isn't so much the beer as contact with the boys.

In today's liturgy we experience the mystery of making contact and living in Christ. In receiving his Word in the Scripture and his Body in the Eucharist, we are united with Christ. But it is a communion, for we are united together by our union with Him. By reciting the "Our Father," on the way to work, while doing housework, while going to school, puts us in contact with Christ and others as well as the Father. The "Our" helps change the "me and God" to "we and God."

It is only by paying attention to someone by really looking at ... really seeing ... really listening to ... really speaking to...that we can have personal contact. When we refuse to have personal contact, we are blocking off the way to have contact with Christ, we are refusing to abide in Him. Whenever we refuse to contact, to see another person, we are blinding ourselves, isolating ourselves, making ourselves less of a person. God has joined us as branches on a vine are joined. A cut off branch does not produce fruit. It dies. A branch in contact grows and bears fruit.

At the annual meeting of the National Hospitals Association in San Francisco recently, one of the speakers gave an illustration that generated a great deal of discussion among the doctors and the nurses present. The speaker told the story of a young nurse who was ministering to a young man her own age. The patient had terminal cancer. The nurse knew that the young man wanted to talk with her but because she was afraid that she wouldn't have the "right answers," and she decided to back off. In her own words "I know he wanted to talk to me, but I always turned it into something light: a little joke or some evasive reassurance, which had to fail. The patient knew, and I knew, but as he saw my desperate attempt to escape, and as

he felt my anxiety, he took pity on me by keeping to himself what he wanted to share with another human being. And so, he died and did not bother me." Christ tells us don't worry about having "the right answers," just let the person talk. Just being present to him, and really listening to him, releases tremendous forces of reassurance within him
- the resurrection power of God within us because the Kingdom of God is within you.

Listening in a caring way can be the greatest gift you can give to anyone. Listening is a way of loving! "I am the Vine, you are the branches." When we give to those who are close to us the feeling that what they think and what they say are worth listening to, we are offering them one of the priceless gifts of love!

"I am the Vine, you are the branches." Incidentally, branches have a certain advantage - they simply have to put to use the food and strength that come from the Vine! We die a little each day in accepting pain and disappointment in order to make room for the Risen life. Christ died to give us life - not in small proportion, but life abundantly.

For this I will praise you Lord in the assembly of your people!

Chapter Ten

DEATH IS DEATH

On the sixth Sunday of Easter April 30, 1978, Monsignor Reynolds preached the following sermon. The readings for that day were (ACTS 8: 5-8, 14-17; 1 PETER 3:15-18; JOHN 14:15-21) (YEAR B).

"I will not leave you orphaned; I will come back to you, a little while now and the world will see me no more! But you see me as one who has life and you will have life" (John 14:19)

A father (whose only daughter was seventeen) was going through a kind of dying. The daughter was preparing to go away to college. Father and daughter had been very close, and he was beginning to feel the pain of separation. They had visited the campus. He had seen the new world she was moving into, and he knew it was not going to be his world anymore. He began to realize that he no longer would be there, as usual, to counsel her and comfort her and protect her. He was finding it difficult to "Let Go." After they had separated for a few days he shed some real tears, but then he was able to reach down to the roots of his Christian faith and move through this experience. He said "I find that because I was able to relinquish her and let go, she started to love me in a new way, and our relationship is better now than ever before. I am now able to rejoice in her discovery of a whole new world, and to my amazement, I find that with my new free time I am able to begin to do some things I had been thinking about for a long time. It is a new life for me. Also, the experience was not only a kind of dying, it was also a resurrection."

That is a very simple incident, nothing startling, quite common. All parents are presented with this sort of challenge, one way or another. But if we see that father's situation in the light of what Jesus is telling us in the Gospels, our lives will never be the same. There is no better way to learn how to do this than to look into John's fourth Gospel.

The Gospel of John divides into two main thrusts, beginning with the story of the wedding at Cana. John presents us with a series of Resurrection signs—Mighty works that Jesus performs, through the miracle of changing water into wine, Jesus is telling us that God is working to transform water into wine, death into life, sorrow into joy, sickness into health. The Resurrection signs continue into chapter Eleven, where the last of the mighty works is recounted: the raising of Lazarus from the dead, a mighty Resurrection sign. During the experience, Jesus says, "I am the Resurrection and the Life." Then the theme breaks and the last half of the Gospel from chapter twelve to the end, concentrates totally on God's supreme sign of the power of His Love; the Death and Resurrection of Jesus Christ Himself. At the pivotal point between these two main sections of John's Gospel, Jesus pronounces a little metaphor so simple that we may tend to gloss over it and miss the profound meaning it has for our lives. Jesus begins talking about His own death. His soul is "troubled," John tells us, He is aware of the enemy moving in, He is aware that if He persists in the things He has been doing, He will soon die. Jesus begins talking about a grain of wheat, a little seed. He says, "Unless the seed dies, there can be no new life." First there must be the death and then the life. This reality is beautifully expressed in these poetic lines:

"Clad in the golds and reds of triumph,

The leaves make the mountains a miracle,

And the valleys a place of wonder,

And yet these leaves are dying, They

are about to flutter from the trees

Down to the waiting earth where, in death They

will become soft mulch,

Brown mold and indistinguishable earth, And

then, new leaves again,

And so they die, refusing to remember with anguish

Other days long ago when they were fresh little tendrils,

Breaking from the bud in the lush warmth of spring,

> Or the summer days when they were green luxuriant foliage, instead, they deck themselves in joy,
>
> Because after the mulch and the mold and the earth,
>
> They will become new leaves again,
>
> This must be the meaning of their reds,
>
> And of their golds."

Jesus tells us to look at the world of nature all around us, what do we see? We see God acting through a process of Death and Resurrection. There are many theories of how life unfolds. There is the theory of "Inevitable Progress;" Day-by-Day, in every way, things will get better and better. There is the Asian theory in which a person goes around and around in circles until his "karma" has built up to the point where he is able to break out of the circle and then as a drop to the ocean, in the absolute, to his god. What Jesus is saying to us in the Gospel of John, however, is that the way life unfolds for nature, for history, for the world, for us as individuals, is through a process of Death and Resurrection. That God is present in every death experience, without exception. That God is working continuously to transform the water into wine, the death into new life.

In order to appreciate this, we must take the death part seriously. The poem about the leaves ends with the leaves dying happy. In the last lines, which I did not read, the poet tells us that we should die happily, therefore. But in the Gospels, we do not see Jesus dying happily. He speaks of the trouble in His soul. We know of His tears and His anguish in Gethsemane. We know of His pain when betrayed and abandoned by His friends. We know of His loneliness when the disciples couldn't stay awake with Him for even an hour. We know the words of utter anguish He spoke from the cross. Death is Death. And we need to understand the pain that is there before we can appreciate the wonder of the Resurrection that follows.

There is the story of two little boys talking about their respective family situations. One of them said "My father is a doctor, I can get sick for nothing." The other boy said, "Big Deal! My daddy is a minister, and I can be good for nothing."

Some of the recent literature on dying would have us believe that death is nothing, that there is no price to pay, that all we need to do is step lightly into the Glory of Life-After-Life — Die Happy! But the New Testament is saying that death is death, after all. Real death, with pain and fear and anxiety and deprivation and anger — all of those very real and human things. But it is also saying, "Praise God and Thank God," because His Resurrection Power is present in that very dying. Praise God and Thank God because when you are feeling most the pain of your dying, you will be closest to Him. As you move through death, God is with you. God is Loving you. God is opening up for you the possibilities of a glorious NEW life.

Saint Paul talks about the death of the body as the culmination of a series of little deaths and resurrections. Paul calls our physical death "the last enemy." It is very real as an enemy for people who love life. There are ways to face it with courage and ultimately with joy- but not with superficial happiness.

There is a haunting story about a wealthy merchant in Baghdad who sent his servant to the market place one morning. There the servant saw the figure of Death moving among the people. Death seemed to look at him very menacingly and the servant became panic stricken. He rushed home and begged his master to give him a horse so that he might leave Baghdad to escape Death. He wanted to flee to a city called Samara. The merchant had pity on his servant and gave him his fastest white Arabian horse, and the servant immediately galloped off for Samara. Later that day, the merchant himself went to the market where he too saw the vision of Death. He approached the figure and asked him why he had stared so threateningly at his servant that morning. Death said to the merchant, "That was not a threatening look, it was a look of surprise. I was surprised to see that man in the city of Baghdad. You see, I have an appointment with him tonight, in the city of Samara."

The story is troubling in one respect. We know that there are some things we can do to delay the appointment with Death. We can fasten our seatbelts, we can get proper exercise and eat the right food. We can stop smoking and so on. There is a dangerous fatalism that comes through in the story when we confront it head-on. But the basic truth it embodies is a truth. We all, ultimately, will have to keep an appointment with Death.

We Die! But the same God who gave us Life in the beginning, gives us New Life in the beauty of our spiritual body.

In today's Gospel lesson, Jesus promises us once more,

"I will not leave you orphaned, I will come back to you... You see me as one who has life, and you will have life... Come then! Let us be on our way." (John 14:18-19,31)

Chapter Eleven

DIVINE GOSSIP

On the Seventh Sunday of Easter May 31, 1981, Monsignor Reynolds preached the following sermon. The readings for that day were (ACTS 1:12-14; 1 PETER 4:13-16; JOHN 17:1-11) (YEAR A).

"Now they realize that all You gave Me comes from You. I entrusted to them the message You entrusted to Me, and they received it. They have known that in truth I came from You, they have believed it was You who sent Me." (JOHN 1:7-8)

A certain town had four churches: Lutheran, Roman Catholic, Methodist, and Baptist. One Spring Day, the four local pastors happened to meet by chance in the village park. They sat on a bench and began to share, in confidence, some of their parish experiences and personal problems. Said the Lutheran Minister, "Perhaps you can help me with a problem I've been having recently. You see I've taken to gambling," This evoked a gasp from the other three. The Roman Catholic Priest said, "I must tell you that lately I have been drinking a little too much." There was a second gasp. The Methodist Minister then said, "Lately I find myself preoccupied with an attractive married woman in the parish." This was followed by a third gasp. Finally, the Baptist Minister said, "I hesitate to tell you this, but my problem is I'm an incurable gossip."

A "Gossip," the dictionary tells us, is one who habitually reveals personal or sensational facts. In this sense, gossiping may be bad, or good. Jesus habitually reveals personal and sensational facts about God, Our Father - all of it good, of course.

Jesus habitually reveals the sensational Good News that God, Our Father, is a gracious God who loves us infinitely and who wants to bring us into union with him. Jesus habitually reveals the sensational Good News of the Father's promise of incredibly joyous New Life to those who trustingly keep His word.

Throughout the Gospel, Jesus prays aloud to the Father. He wants us to overhear, He wants us to spread this Good News out loud.

He prays "I have revealed Your Name, I will continue to reveal it so that your love for Me will live in them (John 12:26) That they may share my Joy completely (John 17:13). In today's Gospel lesson, we overhear Jesus praying to the Father, "I entrusted to them the message You entrusted to Me, and they received it. They have known that in truth I came from You. They have believed it was You who sent Me." (John 17:8) It is all a matter of trust, of believing in God. Our Father, believes in us as worth saving, worth redeeming, worth bringing into union with Himself. God, Our Father, trusts us in a totally life-giving way. Literally, He is offering the gift of His own Life to us in the Person of the Lord, Jesus Christ. It remains for us to believe and trust in the Father in a totally life- giving way. Literally, it remains for us to offer our own life to the Father through the Lord Jesus Christ.

Jesus uses many simple illustrations to teach us that faith, at its heart, is a matter of trusting God. He uses the illustration of little children, of birds in the air, of lilies in the field, to name a few. He tells us to respond to God like the little children, children who are not yet ready to claim independence from their parents. It is essentially an attitude and approach to life which acknowledges that dependence on God and trust in God is where we find our meaning and purpose for living.

A beautiful description of Christian conversion came from a man who said "I have submitted my resignation as manager of the universe and God has accepted it." He did not mean to say that he was withdrawing from the world and its problems. What he meant was that henceforth he was prepared to do things God's way rather than his own way. Henceforth, he would trust God like a little child; henceforth, God's will be done. To become fully human, it is not enough to FEEL you can trust God. To become fully human, it is not enough to SAY you can trust God. To become fully human you must express your TRUST in God concretely in the way you conduct your life. To become fully human you must, in a childlike simplicity, ACCEPT God's will and do it. "He who obeys the commandments he has from Me, is the man who loves Me, and he will be loved by My Father," Jesus says. "This is my command, that you love one another as I have loved you."

The following notice appeared in the "Bargain Hunter's Guide" of a Massachusetts newspaper: "Retired school teacher tired of reading and arithmetic! Is there a gentleman in late 60's or older, who can help me find my way to the playground before the bell rings?"

Jesus is saying "if you want to find your way to the playground before your bell rings, give of yourself to others as I gave of myself to you. I have been there before you. Trust me when I tell you that there is no other way to fulfill yourself as a human person."

Before this week is over, your life will touch the lives of many other people. And in the spirit of trust in God, you can work at creating a relationship that is good; that recognizes the integrity of the other person; that calls forth the unique gifts of the other person; that says to the other person "I care, I really do care."

Some of you may remember several years ago when on Good Friday, a severe earthquake hit Alaska. Many buildings were totally destroyed, including the church of All Saints. Consequently, on Easter Sunday, Parishioners of All Saints went to nearby Saint Mary's Church which had sustained only minor damage. Among the visiting worshipers was an astute and sensitive journalist who reported the experience, he said "We met and worshiped with the Saint Mary's congregation in our "long johns" and slacks in the unheated church. Some burst into tears when they saw friends they had been concerned about; some cried with relief at the sudden awakening out of a state of shock. But no one cried with grief. We sang with gusto and the words of the traditional hymns of Resurrection had a special meaning for us that morning, in the church, that Easter Sunday. There were two lists for the people to fill out. One was headed "We Need," the other was headed "We Have To Share." No one signed the first list. Fifty families signed the second. Listing everything they were willing to share from homes to food, to fireplace wood and labor. Some of those who signed this second list had lost virtually everything they had except the things they listed to share. This was indeed the

Church of Christ on the morning of the Third Day."

The Divine Gossip has it that Almighty God's Resurrection Power is present to you, to the Church, to the family, to the nation, to the world offering new life and new hope, if only you will hear and obey in simple trust.

A woman attended a meeting where she met her former high school music teacher whom she hadn't seen for over thirty years. She introduced herself and then went on to recall how much extra time and encouragement the teacher had given her, "I was so inspired by you," she said, "that I decided to continue my music education in college and graduate school. Now I am a college professor and the head of the entire music department." Later as they said their "goodbyes," the teacher said to her former pupil, "Thank you for saying all those nice things about my teaching, you have made my day." The woman replied, "Oh No, let me thank you, you've made my life!"

The DIVINE GOSSIP has it that to make your life, you've got to share it!

Chapter Twelve

FEELINGS

On Pentecost Sunday MAY 14, 1978, Monsignor Reynolds preached the following sermon. The readings for that day were (ACTS 2:1-11; 1 CORINTHIANS 12:3-7, 12-13; JOHN 20:19-23) (YEAR A).

"Jesus came and stood before them. "Peace be with you," He said. At the sight of the Lord the Disciples Rejoiced." (JOHN 20: 19-20)

In the Old Testament saga, Israel's greatest King is David. He was called the "Lion of Judah," the "Warrior King." David was a great military leader. He had great expertise in financial affairs. He was a great organizer and administrator. He was King of Israel during her "Golden Age." In fact, he was largely responsible for bringing it about. It was almost 3000 years ago when King David put together a parade the likes of which have never been seen since, not even on our modern TV screens.

David, after overcoming many obstacles, had established Jerusalem as the Capital City, the "Holy City." He had built the great wall around the city. He had built the water supply system. He had devised the military defenses for the city. He had been able to do many other marvelous things to make the city great! But there was one thing missing: The Ark of the Covenant. The Ark of the Covenant, from earliest times in their history, was for the Hebrew people a symbol of God's presence in their midst. It was their Holiest symbol. When they had wandered through the desert, the Ark of the Covenant was there to remind them that because God was with them, they would reach the Promised Land. When they had wondered why His Chosen People had to suffer so many hardships and disappointments, the Ark of the Covenant was there to remind them of His great love for them and His promise of their fulfillment. They had carried the Ark of the Covenant with them into battle as a sign of God's presence in the midst of their struggle. There was no way, therefore, that Jerusalem could really be the Capital of the City until the Ark of the Covenant was safely enshrined within its walls. Finally, King David was able to bring the Ark of the Covenant into the Holy City, and that is when he organized the big parade.

David placed the Ark of the Covenant in an Ox-drawn cart. He placed all of his best musicians out in front, with their tambourines and cymbals and castanets and other instruments. He had all the people lined up and following behind, joining in the great parade formation. Then the Great King David felt such joy, such ecstasy, such deep feelings of praise and thanksgiving to God, that he took off his clothes and dressed only in the briefest loin cloth, performed an uninhibited wild "Zorba-The-Greek" like dance before the people. It was his way of saying "God, this is the way I feel about you today, I cannot keep it to myself, I will not let anything people might say prevent me from expressing my feelings about you today God." (Indeed, David's wife, looking down on the scene from the palace, most emphatically disapproved of what she saw).

What does this biblical episode have to say about our life in today's world? To understand this, we must first of all appreciate who David was. He was a practical and reasonable man, to be sure. If he were not, he could not have given his people the kind of leadership which he did, in the military, economic, and political sense. He was a wise King capable of making the tough decisions that had to be made. But David was also a feeling man. There were times in his relationship with others when he expressed deep grief. David knew how to cry. There were times, in his relationships with others, when he expressed deep remorse for sinning against them. There were times, in his relationships with others, when he expressed bitterness and anger and frustration. But not only did he do this in his human relationships, he did it in his relationship with God.

There is the story of a woman choir member who came to church each Sunday with her three children and her father. She would take her place in the choir loft, and the children would sit in a pew with the grandfather. He was a man who loved going to church on Sunday. Especially, he loved the preaching and when something was said that really turned him on, he would express himself out loud, "Hallelujah!" he would shout, or "Praise the Lord!" Once he was even heard to say "Right On!" These outbursts became increasingly embarrassing to his daughter, the choir member. Finally, she confronted him with her problem saying, "Dad, I know your feelings are sincere, but when you cry out in Church as you do, it is embarrassing to me, and think of the children, how embarrassing it is to them! I wish you would try not to do this any more. Your birthday is coming soon and, if you'll try very hard for the next month not to create a disturbance in Church, you'll be sure to get those new hunting boots you've wanted for so long." The following Sunday all went well, although the sermon was a fiery as ever, the old man remained silent. On the second Sunday, however, the preacher was talking about God's grace and God's love with a passion. He said that God's love for us is great; that He draws near to us in Jesus Christ; that God Himself has come to us in Jesus Christ to tell us that He loves us; that God offers us through Jesus Christ, wholeness of life and Joy; that through Jesus Christ, God makes sense for us out of this tangled existence of ours. Hearing all of this, poor old grandfather became more and more excited until he reached the point where he simply could not restrain himself any longer, "boots or no boots" he cried out, "Hallelujah!"

Would that more of us could share that deep feeling of joy and somehow express it? Week after week many of us, when we hear this Good News say to ourselves, "It sounds like a good idea, I'll have to think about that during the coming week." But we're not feeling the Word of God. We're not actually experiencing it down at the deepest level of our being. Consequently, we are unable to rejoice over this great Good News God is giving us.

In today's Gospel lesson, Jesus reveals the Good News of the Resurrection Power of God. He appears as the Risen Lord to His frightened disciples saying "Peace be with you! ... Peace be with you!" He is telling the disciples that He has Risen in order to bring them peace, to bring them to fulfillment, to make their lives whole and complete. Everlastingly, whole, and complete. And how do they receive this Good News? In the sacred authors own words, "They rejoiced." They didn't say to themselves, "That sounds good, we'll think about it." They didn't receive it as an idea. They didn't intellectualize it. Having received the Holy Spirit of God deep within their souls, the Disciples "Rejoiced." The Apostle John has captured the real meaning of the Pentecost event no less for us than for the Disciples in Jesus' time. Inside we have deep, deep feelings about God.

So, Tell Him!

Express your feelings to God! Let Him in your life, at the deepest level of your being.

Just as He worked in the lives of the Disciples in the upper room; just as He worked in the life of David, "The Dancing King," express freely and unreservedly your love for God and you will discover by the power of His Holy Spirit, how to express freely and unreservedly your love for one another.

"May the Peace of Christ Be with You Always." (2 Thessalonians 3:16)

AFTERWORD

The Life and Legacy of Monsignor James B. Reynolds

Monsignor James Bernard Reynolds lived his priesthood as an act of joyful invitation. For more than seven decades, he sought to draw people together-not only to worship, but to one another-believing that community itself could be a pathway to God.

Born on January 18, 1925, in Brooklyn, New York, to James and Kathleen Reynolds, first-generation Irish immigrants, he was one of three children raised in a home shaped by faith, hard work, and humor. Long before his ordination, he supported himself through a variety of jobs-from ushering at Ebbets Field to working in machine shops, retail, and travel services. As a young seminarian, he spent summers as a tour guide on New York City sightseeing buses, a role that foreshadowed both his love of storytelling and his lifelong conviction that leading people-anywhere-was a sacred trust.

He entered Immaculate Conception Seminary in Huntington, Long Island, in 1946 and was ordained to the priesthood for the Diocese of Brooklyn on June 3, 1950. He would later say that he was drawn to the priesthood by the evident joy of priests he admired, and that seeing Going My Way, with Bing Crosby, confirmed his sense that faith and warmth need not be at odds. "In leading people to exciting locations on earth," he once reflected, "I thought I might someday escort people to heaven—and manage perhaps to get in through a side door myself."

Monsignor Reynolds served for sixteen years in the Diocese of Brooklyn before relocating to South Florida in 1966 on medical advice, hoping the climate would ease recurring pleurisy. He was welcomed into the Archdiocese of Miami in 1970, where he would spend the remainder of his active ministry. Along the way, he earned master's degrees in psychological counseling and religious education, bringing both intellectual depth and pastoral sensitivity to his work.

His assignments reflected the breadth of his service: parochial vicar, administrator, spiritual director, diocesan office director, chaplain, and moderator for lay organizations. He served at parishes including Holy Rosary (now Holy Rosary–St. Richard), Annunciation, Nativity, Holy Spirit, St. James in North Miami, and most notably, St. Henry Catholic Church in Pompano Beach, where he was pastor for twenty-five years.

It was at St. Henry that Monsignor Reynolds gave fullest expression to his belief that a parish should function not merely as a congregation, but as a family-one that prayed, worked, and recreated together. In 1984, with the blessing of Archbishop Edward A. McCarthy, he founded Henry's Hideaway, a parish-based supper club that quickly became legendary. Designed especially for older parishioners-whom he affectionately called "chronologically gifted"- the club offered professional entertainers, music, laughter, fellowship, and dignity. It welcomed people of all faiths and backgrounds and became, in his words, "a pastoral experiment in creating community."

Travel was another extension of his pastoral vision. He led parish trips to destinations near and far, served regularly as a cruise-ship chaplain, and delighted in the metaphor of journeying together—geographically and spiritually. Even in leisure, he remained a shepherd.

Monsignor Jim periodically served as a cruise ship priest with an organization called Apostleship of the Sea of the USA. Aboard the cruise ship he had the opportunity to meet various entertainers and would invite them back to Henry's Hideaway for a Saturday night gig. As the tuxedo-clad master of ceremonies (MC), Monsignor Jim opened every Saturday night at Henry's Hideaway after the 5:00pm Mass when he sang, joked, and mingled through the crowd. After dinner was served, he then introduced the performers with unmistakable delight. Following the show, a band started playing for dancing until closing time. Over time, Henry's Hideaway grew to nearly a thousand members and hosted dozens of Big Band, Broadway, and Las Vegas-style acts each year. His "MC" role also earned him a collection of affectionate nicknames: "Mr. Saturday Night," "Gangplank Jim," "Father Daddy-O," and thanks to his signature phrase-simply, "Baby, Baby."

Yet beneath the wit and showmanship was a priest deeply serious about kindness. He rejected the notion that priests should stand above others and believed instead that authentic ministry required accessibility, humility, and genuine interest in people's lives. Those who met him often remarked that he had the rare gift of making each person feel uniquely seen and remembered. As an example, Monsignor Jim, officiating at my wedding, at the time of making our vows, stood below our floor level and had us face the wedding guests. That definitely made us uniquely seen and remembered and was very special.

In 1997, in recognition of his service, Archbishop John C. Favalora named him a Monsignor. He retired from active parish leadership in 2005 but remained closely connected to friends, parishioners, and clergy colleagues. He lived for six months with me in Saint Augustine, Florida shortly after his eightieth birthday and his formal retirement before eventually moving to California to be near my cousins.

Monsignor James B. Reynolds died on February 28, 2022, in Laguna Niguel, California, at the age of ninety-seven, surrounded by loved ones. He was survived by four nieces (I being one of his nieces), five nephews, and great-nieces and nephews spread across the United States-along with countless spiritual sons and daughters whose lives were touched by his ministry. He baptized me and was my priest for two of my marriages and was my confessor on occasion. "Have priest will travel" was my motto for him. I am sure he presided over many sacraments for my cousins families as well, including giving last rites and officiating at funerals. In my opinion, he always was a giver of his time, talents, and treasure.

While in Laguna Niguel, he lived for a few years in my cousin's home. There he would say Daily Mass. On May 12, 2022, not even three months after his death, my cousins neighborhood experienced a horrific wildfire, consuming homes burned to the ground in Coronado Pointe. It made national news. And of course, my first instinct was to contact my cousin. I was relieved to learn that my cousins house was spared except for smoke damage. The houses to the right, left and across the street were also untouched except for smoke damage. Twenty others succumbed to the devastation of the wildfire. When I viewed the aerial pictorial position of their house, it seemed to me to form part of a cross + (the backside of the cross fell off to a canyon). Houses next to the four spared houses had burned to the ground. It is my personal humble opinion and belief that their home was saved as a "Monsignor Jim miracle" on my cousins' behalf because of the sacredness of having had Daily Mass said in their home by him for so many years. I look forward to the day when I can ask him, "did you help to do that?"

When asked to describe the ideal priest, Jim swiftly answered with a single word: kindness. That word remains an apt summary of his legacy. Through sermons and songs, laughter and listening, parish halls and sanctuaries, Monsignor Jim preached the Gospel not only from the pulpit, but from the dance floor, the dinner table, and the quiet places of human encounter.

During younger years I recall in his rare "free-time," he would swim in the Atlantic Ocean and swim for what seemed like miles. I asked him once what he was thinking while swimming. He replied he didn't "think" of anything because that is when he would say the Rosary, all mysteries, and all decades.

While Monsignor was living with me, I vividly recall a conversation about how he felt about his priesthood. He actually said that he feared dying. When I asked him why he felt that way, he humbly said "I don't think I have done enough work for God." Of course, he was only 80 then and lived another 17 years after that comment. Well, I'm pretty confident he made it all the way to heaven through the front gate not the side door.

With all the joy in heaven, one can imagine he has already gathered a crowd—welcoming everyone in, smiling broadly, greeting them all with "Baby, Baby" and bursting into song, singing Mac the Knife or New York, New York, and gently and joyfully reminding them that faith is meant to be lived together.

Rev. Msgr. James B. Reynolds
October 26, 1997

The biographical afterword in this volume is an original work based on publicly available obituary notices published by the Archdiocese of Miami and Dignity Memorial, as well as personal recollections.

Artificial intelligence tools were used as a writing and editorial aid in the drafting and refinement of some of this material. All final content, interpretation, and editorial decisions are solely the responsibility of the editor.

Similar research and writing practices may be used in later volumes in this series.

ACKNOWLEDGEMENTS

Special thanks to my cousins for helping with the clearance from Monsignor's estate to write this book. I also warmly thank all six of my cousins, who cheerfully cared for Monsignor for seventeen years during his retirement and especially in his final days by including him in their families and activities.

With great appreciation to Cris Leone for his editorial review and comments.

Another incredibly special note of gratitude to Archbishop Thomas Wenski of the Archdiocese of Miami, Florida, for his participation in the concelebration at Monsignor's funeral on March 11, 2022, and for his encouraging words to me in compiling and writing this book.

Kathleen M. Hackett

Ponte Vedra Beach, Florida 2026

Made in the USA
Coppell, TX
19 February 2026

72000752R00069